Blake Griffin

By Jon M. Fishman

AMAZING ATHLETES

Lerner Publications Company • Minneapolis

Lerner Publications Company
A division of Lerner Publishing Group, Inc.
241 First Avenue North
Minneapolis, MN 55401 USA

For reading levels and more information, look up this title at www.lernerbooks.com.

Library of Congress Cataloging-in-Publication Data

Fishman, Jon M.
    Blake Griffin / by Jon M. Fishman.
    pages   cm. — (Amazing athletes)
    Includes index.
    ISBN 978–1–4677–4505–5 (lib. bdg. : alk. paper)
    ISBN 978–1–4677–4581–9 (eBook)
    1. Griffin, Blake, 1989-—Juvenile literature. 2. Basketball players—United States—Biography—Juvenile literature. I. Title.
    GV884.G76F57 2015
    796.323092—dc23 [B]   2014002546

Manufactured in the United States of America
1 – BP – 7/15/14

TABLE OF CONTENTS

Blake Griffin soars to the basket on January 10, 2014.

"DOING EVERYTHING"

Blake Griffin of the Los Angeles Clippers raced to the basket. His teammate Darren Collison had the ball. Blake and Collison made eye contact. Then Collison lofted the ball near the basket. Blake leaped. He grabbed the ball in midair and slammed it through the basket. **Alley-oop!**

Blake and the Clippers were playing against the Los Angeles Lakers on January 10, 2014. The Clippers were playing without superstar **point guard** Chris Paul. Lakers **shooting guard** Kobe Bryant was also out with an injury.

The Clippers and the Lakers both play their home games at Staples Center in Los Angeles. But the two teams have vastly different histories. The Lakers have won the National Basketball Association (NBA) championship 16 times. Only the Boston Celtics have more titles. The Clippers have never won a championship. The Clippers wanted to prove that history didn't matter on January 10. With Paul

Blake looks down the court to plan his next move.

Blake (*right*) blocks a shot attempted by Lakers player Wesley Johnson (*left*).

and Bryant both on the bench, all eyes were on Blake. He took over the game in the second half. Blake plays **power forward**. This position offers plenty of chances to score. He threw down **slam dunks** as other players scrambled out of his way. He scored with long shots away from the basket. He also made sharp passes to teammates and played tough defense.

The Clippers won the game, 123–87. Blake had 33 points. He also grabbed 12 **rebounds** and chipped in four **assists**. The win gave the Clippers 26 wins and just 13 losses for the season.

The Clippers used to play in San Diego, California. The team moved to Los Angeles in 1984.

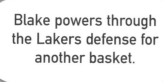
Blake powers through the Lakers defense for another basket.

Blake led the Clippers to their big win against the Lakers.

Fans know Blake as a high-flying dunker. But he has to play well in all aspects of the game for the Clippers to win. "Blake is doing everything for us, rebounding and defending," said Clippers coach Doc Rivers. "He is a great passer. It gets lost in his fancy dunks."

Blake grew up in Oklahoma City, Oklahoma.

GROWING UP GRIFFIN

Blake Austin Griffin was born in Oklahoma City, Oklahoma, on March 16, 1989. His brother, Taylor, is about three years older. The two were a close pair from the beginning. They loved to spend time together horsing around. They also tried to beat each other at whatever they were doing.

"Everything Blake did, he made it into a game, a challenge," said Gail, the boys' mom.

But Blake had a hard time keeping pace with Taylor. "He was three years older, so he was bigger, stronger, and faster," Blake said. "I was always one step behind."

Blake *(second from left)* is close to his brother *(left)*, father *(second from right)*, and mother *(right)*.

Taylor and Blake could also work as a team, though. Their father, Tommy, is a high school math teacher and basketball coach. Gail is a former high school teacher. But

Blake's favorite TV show is *Saturday Night Live*. "Oh, man, I would love to host that show someday," he said.

Taylor and Blake didn't go to school until they were teenagers. Instead, Gail taught her sons at home. The boys learned together and played together.

In 2003, Blake enrolled in nearby Oklahoma Christian School (OCS) as a freshman. Taylor was starting his third year at OCS. Their dad was the school's head basketball coach.

The Griffins helped make the OCS Saints basketball team unbeatable. They won game after game. In March 2004, the Saints made it to the state championship. They hadn't lost all season. The title game took place at Oklahoma State Fair Arena in Oklahoma City. It was close, but OCS came out on top, 55–50. They were a perfect 29–0 for the season.

Winning the state championship was great for Blake and his teammates. But Taylor was the star of the team. Blake was too young to play much. So he watched and learned from his brother. Soon his patience would pay off.

Many events take place at Oklahoma State Fair Arena, including high school basketball games like this one.

Blake's brother, Taylor Griffin *(left)*, slips past University of Memphis guard Jeremy Hunt *(right)* during a college game.

FOUR-TIME CHAMP

The Saints won the state tournament again in 2005. Taylor was still the team's star player. But it was his final year of high school. When he moved on to the University of Oklahoma (OU), it was Blake's time to shine for OCS.

The 2005–2006 season was another success. Once again, the OCS Saints had the best basketball team in the state. Once again, they won the state tournament. But this time, Blake led the way.

By the start of Blake's senior year, it was clear that he was the best **amateur** basketball player in Oklahoma. Many people thought he was one of the best in the country. In a 2006–2007 game against Southeast High School, he scored an incredible 41 points. He also snagged 28 rebounds and passed for 10 assists.

In 2007, Blake played in the McDonald's All American Game. This is a game for the best high school basketball seniors from around the country. Blake was well known for his ability to soar above the basket. He agreed to compete in the event's slam dunk contest.

Blake *(left)* leaps up to dunk the ball during the 2007 McDonald's All American Game.

Blake threw down a variety of dunks in the contest. For his best slam, he stood near the **free-throw line** with his back to the basket. He bounced the ball between his legs and off the backboard. Blake twisted and grabbed the ball in the air. He spun his arm like a windmill and smashed the ball through the hoop. His teammates went wild. They stormed the court to celebrate the vicious dunk. Blake was named the winner of the contest.

Blake was named to the Oklahoma Boys All-State Basketball Team after the season. He had averaged 28.6 points, 15.1 rebounds, and 4.9 assists per game for the year. Even better, OCS won the state tournament for the fourth year in a row with Blake on the team.

Blake wasn't the only future NBA player on the 2007 McDonald's All American Game team. Superstars such as Kevin Love and Derrick Rose were also on the roster.

Blake *(right)* and brother Taylor *(left)* answer questions at a news conference.

SOONER PRIDE

Oklahoma basketball fans waited anxiously to find out where Blake would play after high school. Blake had many options. Colleges all around the country wanted the big man known for ferocious slam dunks.

Meanwhile, Taylor was enjoying his time at the University of Oklahoma. He knew that his basketball coach, Jeff Capel, was working hard to build a strong team. Taylor also knew that Capel had his eye on Blake. Taylor encouraged Blake to play for OU. "He said he believed in what Coach Capel was doing," Blake said. That was good enough for the younger Griffin. Blake started school at OU in the fall of 2007.

Brothers Blake *(left)* and Taylor *(right)* practice together at the University of Oklahoma.

The Oklahoma Sooners have a long history of basketball excellence. But the previous season had been a tough one. The Sooners finished with a record of 16–15. They missed the **National Collegiate Athletic Association (NCAA) tournament**.

Adding Blake to the team made a difference right away. He averaged more than 14 points and almost 10 rebounds per game in

Blake takes a shot for the Oklahoma Sooners.

2007–2008. The team advanced to the second round of the NCAA tournament. But they seemed overmatched against the University of Louisville. OU lost the game by 30 points, 78–48.

Blake grabs a rebound during the NCAA tournament.

Despite the loss, Blake had made his mark as a standout player. As soon as the game was over, people started asking Blake about his future.

Taylor Griffin had a very short NBA career. He played eight games for the Phoenix Suns in 2009–2010.

He stood 6 feet 10 inches tall and was packed full of muscles. Many basketball insiders thought he could be chosen in the first round of that year's NBA **draft**. But in April 2008, Blake announced that he'd be back at OU for at least one more year.

Blake and his teammates advanced deep into the NCAA tournament in 2009. They finally lost to the University of North Carolina, 72–60. Blake had done all he could with 23 points and 16 rebounds.

Blake receives his award after being named the Associated Press College Basketball Player of the Year.

FROM OKLAHOMA TO LOS ANGELES

The 2008–2009 season had been the best yet for Blake. He received a slew of prizes. Among them was the Associated Press College Basketball Player of the Year trophy.

Blake *(left)* was one of the best players on the Oklahoma Sooners throughout his college career.

The OU men's basketball team had greatly improved in the past couple of seasons. Someone asked Coach Capel what advice he'd give other coaches to help their teams. "Easy," said Capel with a smile. "Get a guy like Blake Griffin."

Blake decided it was time to move on to the NBA. On June 25, 2009, he was chosen first in the draft by the Los Angeles Clippers. The team and their fans were thrilled to have such an exciting young player join the team. But the feeling didn't last long. Blake hurt his knee before the season even started. He had surgery and would be out for a year.

Mike Dunleavy Sr. was the Clippers coach at the time. He talked about how much the team would miss Blake. "It's a little disappointing, because he brings so much to the table," Coach Dunleavy said.

Blake applies ice to his injured knee during a Clippers game.

After recovering from his injury, Blake was back in action for the 2010–2011 season.

In 2010–2011, Blake showed the world that the injury was no longer slowing him down. He was back at full strength and crushing slam dunks as only he can. Since he didn't play at all in 2009–2010, Blake was still considered a rookie. He was the obvious choice for NBA Rookie of the Year. He won in a landslide vote.

"When I got injured, I just decided I had to come back even better," Blake said. "I had to keep improving even while I couldn't play, and I dedicated myself to that."

Blake agreed to dunk in the NBA slam dunk contest at the 2011 All-Star Game. He won the contest, just as he did in high school four years earlier.

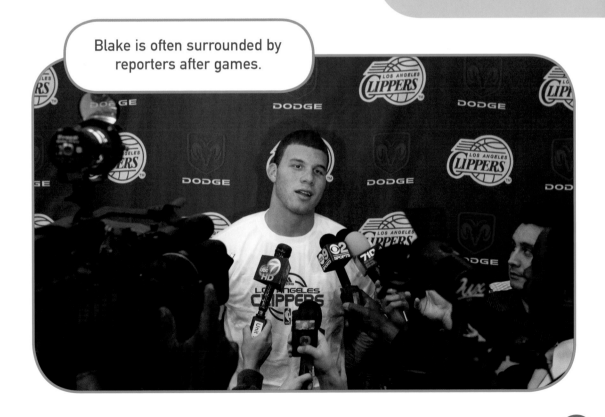

Blake is often surrounded by reporters after games.

In four NBA seasons, Blake has averaged about 20 points and 10 rebounds per game. He's been named to multiple **All-Star Games**. He's also provided some of the most exciting highlights NBA fans have ever seen.

Blake *(right)* signs autographs for excited fans.

Selected Career Highlights

2013–2014 Named to the NBA All-Star Game for the fourth time

2012–2013 Named to the NBA All-Star Game for the third time
Finished tied for 19th in the NBA in rebounds per game (8.3)
Finished 19th in the NBA in points per game (18)

2011–2012 Named to the NBA All-Star Game for the second time
Finished sixth in the NBA in rebounds per game (10.9)
Finished 10th in the NBA in points per game (20.7)

2010–2011 Named NBA Rookie of the Year
Named to the NBA All-Star Game for the first time
Finished fourth in the NBA in rebounds per game (12.1)
Finished 12th in the NBA in points per game (22.5)

2009–2010 Missed the season with a knee injury
Drafted first overall by the Clippers

2008–2009 Helped OU reach the fourth round of the NCAA tournament

2007–2008 Helped OU reach the second round of the NCAA tournament

2006–2007 Won the state championship at OCS for the fourth straight year
Won McDonald's All American Game's slam dunk contest

2005–2006 Won the state championship at OCS for the third straight year

2004–2005 Won the state championship at OCS for the second straight year

2003–2004 Won the state championship at OCS

Glossary

alley-oop: a play where a high pass is thrown to a player who catches the ball in midair and dunks it

All-Star Games: midseason games played by the best players in the NBA. Fans vote to decide who plays in an All-Star Game.

amateur: someone who does an activity for fun, without being paid

assists: passes to teammates that help them score baskets

draft: a yearly event in which sports teams take turns choosing new players

free-throw line: a line near the basket at each end of a basketball court. Free throws are taken from behind the free-throw line.

National Collegiate Athletic Association (NCAA) tournament: a yearly tournament in which 65 teams compete to decide the national champion

point guard: a player who is responsible for running the team's offensive plays. Point guards are skilled at dribbling and passing the ball.

power forward: a player who usually plays close to the basket. Power forwards must be skilled at scoring and rebounding.

rebounds: balls caught after shots to the basket are missed

shooting guard: a player who is mainly responsible for scoring. Shooting guards are skilled at scoring in a number of ways.

slam dunks: shots in which players forcefully slam the ball through the hoop

Further Reading & Websites

Kennedy, Mike, and Mark Stewart. *Swish: The Quest for Basketball's Perfect Shot*. Minneapolis: Millbrook Press, 2009.

NBA Website
http://www.nba.com
The NBA's website provides fans with news, statistics, biographies of players and coaches, and information about games.

Official Site of the Los Angeles Clippers
http://www.nba.com/clippers
The official website of the Clippers includes schedules, news, and profiles of past and current players and coaches.

Savage, Jeff. *Kobe Bryant*. Minneapolis: Lerner Publications, 2011.

Sports Illustrated Kids
http://www.sikids.com
The *Sports Illustrated Kids* website covers all sports, including basketball.

LERNER
SOURCE

Expand learning beyond the printed book. Download free, complementary educational resources for this book from our website, www.lernerresource.com.

Index

Photo Acknowledgments

The images in this book are used with the permission of: AP Photo/Mark J.
Terrill, pp. 4, 7, 26, 29; © EPA/Paul Buck/Alamy, p. 6; © Rose Palmisano/The
Orange County Register/ZUMAPRESS.com/Alamy, p. 8; © EPA/Paul Buck/
Alamy, p. 9; © iStockphoto.com/Justin Voight, p. 10; AP Photo/Sue Ogrocki,
pp. 11, 28; AP Photo, p. 13; AP Photo/Michael Conroy, p. 14; © Andy Lyons/
Getty Images, p. 16; AP Photo/Orlin Wagner, p. 18; AP Photo/The Oklahoman,
Steve Sisney, p. 19; AP Photo/James Schammerhorn, p. 20; AP Photo/Jeff
Roberson, p. 21; AP Photo/Paul Sancya, p. 23; AP Photo/Rob Aydelotte, p. 24;
AP Photo/Kevin Terrell, p. 25; AP Photo/Damian Dovarganes, p. 27.

Front cover: © John Green/Cal Sport Media/ZUMAPRESS.com/Newscom.

Main body text set in Caecilia LT Std 55 Roman 16/28.
Typeface provided by Adobe Systems.